MERE EXTINCTION

POEMS

EVIE CHRISTIE

ECW

Published by ECW Press
665 Gerrard Street East
Toronto, Ontario, Canada M4M 1Y2
416-694-3348 / info@ecwpress.com

MISFIT

Editor for the Press: Michael Holmes/
a misFit Book
Cover design: Natalie Olson
Author photo: Evie Christie

LIBRARY AND ARCHIVES CANADA CATALOGUING IN PUBLICATION

Title: Mere extinction : poems / Evie Christie.

Names: Christie, Evie, 1979- author.

Identifiers: Canadiana (print) 20200403192 | Canadiana (ebook) 20200403222

ISBN 978-1-77041-546-1 (softcover)
ISBN 978-1-77305-681-4 (ePUB)
ISBN 978-1-77305-682-1 (PDF)
ISBN 978-1-77305-683-8 (Kindle)

Classification: LCC PS8605.H745 M47 2021 | DDC C811/.6—dc23)

The publication of *Mere Extinction* has been generously supported by the Canada Council for the Arts and is funded in part by the Government of Canada. *Nous remercions le Conseil des arts du Canada de son soutien. Ce livre est financé en partie par le gouvernement du Canada.* We acknowledge the support of the Ontario Arts Council (OAC), an agency of the Government of Ontario, which last year funded 1,965 individual artists and 1,152 organizations in 197 communities across Ontario for a total of $51.9 million. We also acknowledge the contribution of the Government of Ontario through the Ontario Book Publishing Tax Credit, and through Ontario Creates for the marketing of this book.

ONTARIO CREATES

ONTARIO ARTS COUNCIL
CONSEIL DES ARTS DE L'ONTARIO
an Ontario government agency
un organisme du gouvernement de l'Ontario

Canada Council for the Arts
Conseil des Arts du Canada
Canada

PRINTED AND BOUND IN CANADA

PRINTING: COACH HOUSE 5 4 3 2 1

Table of Contents

For my children

Species That Went Extinct Last Year and Some Who Just Died

For Rani Rivera

That one on the park bench by your old apartment we used
to see, cut eying the sun's rise as we left for class. My back
molar next to the real back one, took in my youth, bone
fragments emerged at the wall of flesh for a while.

There were a bunch of birds as well—the sea
was really fucked I heard. Wild water buffalo, no, not quite,
a barbaric will to be keeps 4000 of their hearts beating. Will they go
without anesthesia; why haven't they learned the way? Maybe
they're stupid.

A lot of people-I-know-on-Facebook's dogs and cats.
You. You, in flames, lit up. Shirking the fight. Taking in the light, blue
and infinite. Resting in the everlasting arms, armchairs, futons
while we sit in wait until global warming
or whatever else they've got, winks
in our direction. Let us be more. Make better ones of us.

They say the Asian elephant's DNA goes back to the woolly
mammoth. Maybe.
Let the next ones use our bones for something useful and move on
without us.

When Your Baby Dies (Steps for New Parents)

When your children die of diseases you hadn't heard of
you take off all of your clothes,
you pluck the full red face
from each Bay Flowers poppy and place them around the body.
You play
John Prine, you play Guns N' Roses, Leonard Cohen, Hank Williams's
Lost Highway.

When your baby dies you drink an entire bottle of champagne and tell the funeral home director
to *fuck the fuck off*, that they'll have a body when you're good and ready.
You lie beside them one more night and bathe them and dress them
and you know what cold is the way your ancestors did, the way
your parents never did. What did they give up for the television sitcom?
You dress, clip your stockings at the thigh, pin
a brooch, take a big black Buick to St. James Town and beg
the youngish guy in a suit that used to fit him to be gentle. *It's just a job to him,*
you think, *they probably flip them on the trolley and take a smoke break. It's all a big joke.*
"No, we're gentle," he says.

You march back over at ungodly hours and demand
to hold your child again and again until they realize you're a fucking lunatic.
His face has changed, they will warn; say: *your face will change, too*
and they'll let you in again.

A month from now you'll kiss a stranger on a Bloor West balcony
or find salvation in the strip club blow your Ph.D. friends bring by.
    Colour your hair
and take 5000 selfies. But that's too far away to see right now. Now,

you bring things to be burned with baby.
You stand with the 79-year-old man in the ghetto
that's being eaten alive by goddamn yuppies and when he asks if
    you are sure
you can pull the switch and keep it pulled, you say *yes sir*. You ask
for every piece of bone and he does his best.
You hum your way through the thicket of high-rises, The Halifax,
    The Montreal,
the fruit stand and food bank, the one between Food Basics and
    the community centre?
And someone says, *Hey mama!*
Hey mama you look good today! Wave with the hand
not holding the soot that was your first son
And say *thank you*.

Captains of Industry

Where will you go, our almost young men?
Where, my boyfriend's brothers, my boys' dads, love-
sick and neglected sons of single moms—where
in the late afternoon's horn heavy
intersections will you go? Parliament is open.
Parliament is an open gash and Bleeker sits and waits
like a husband in a maternity ward who's just plain fucking done
waiting. Who's smoked the last of whatever he smokes. Where
my buzz-cutted, hope-waned darlings,
will they find you, your babies, your girls, late evening
when the street lights light
their full and happy faces, their accidental existences, almost pink
and bring you once more, between chop and grab, home.
And where, when you've visited the bare-knuckled bankers of King
Street
and the meat-eating Annex Vegans, where between
the out of milk mothers and the part-time suppliers am I,
my captain, my love, and should I wait up and will you be hungry
and is it some dream?

For Girls Who Sleep with Old Men Who Sleep with Ghosts (A Manual)

There is no room in bed amongst the suicidal schoolboys, perched
by his heroic chest all night. Dead boys' rooms mustn't be filled!
(This is a clause built into particular boyhoods.)

Oh, the white-hot youth-
fulness of girls who pressed their cool, dairy
thighs at him and said, no. The ones he didn't want
when he wanted others, those are the meanest ghosts.
Some are still alive. Look out for them.

Some are fathers, they are trapped inside 12 memories, none of
  their own choosing!
There is working, dying, a glimpse
inside a road trip (split seconds), a ruthlessly domestic hotel room,
  smoke—foreign
habit, fostering abstract loss, going away and away and almost
knowing them. Never knowing them.
Love. Coming home. Work.

Ghosts know what they want. They'll tell you—his prettiest ones,
freighted under long-lashed glances—they'll press
their dead-thick lips to yours and say:
he's an old man and he sleeps with ghosts,
he's more us than he is you.

You'll learn to leave, little girl. Back to your throbbing world with you!
That empire of beating hearts, squandered in a green-drunk
  wilderness.

Bog Girl

After Seamus Heaney

I waited too long, was left waiting
and here I am in my fruit-white youth,
too young to go untouched, a balmy small-town dream
touched up with pink where it mattered.

Remember the ways you wanted to touch and did not
and finally broke in through the window and did
until I got smart and found their sophistication: loveless bliss,
made over and over 'til the earth packed under my nails
was gone. Find me here, waiting, gone blue and winter cold,
make out my parts from the windowsill,
not gleaming, all the same, the same as ever.

Birthright

For Jules Lewis

A hare caught cross-hatched in someone's great grandfather's eye
wasn't it. A great bear cracked open for a deep freezer, a blue-born
    baby,
this astigmatism, flocks of grief, a wilderness of grief, your great,
great grandmother's migraines, this body—
they can't tell you anything.

The hinge swung and both parts parted, my past
and me, the empty fist of time and space choked me,
and drowned me and beat me free
of my ancestry, of the faces in photographs who looked a little like
me. One afternoon I lay against my grandfather's chest, before
rigor mortis set in, and one evening I dressed my baby
for the furnace. They were the same moment.

And many other times, I walked away from you
and him and him and each time the moment was repeated
and had stamped upon itself, itself. Each time the snare's cord
was less so and I was almost alone and it was vast.

This story about how your parents met, a common
middle name, the illness born of Ashkenazi blood, none of these,
not the bear your uncle blasted the teeth from in front of your eyes,
or the headaches inherited like an overvalued wedding ring,
can tell you anything about me now. I'm the hare,
twitching and mindless in a scope, escaping or not,
lucky-footed or chained to a key, peeled or whole,
almost weightless.

Vincent Gallo, Tom Thomson Where Are You

Out here the birds will eat
right outta your hands, they told me.
I eyed the septic bed, jack pines in arabesque, barn,
and decided it was cheap enough.

I'd been eating like a bird
too, in the city, my heart thrashed under an H&M sweater,
as the robin's now throbbed under a robe of feathers in my hand—
I held it in my fingers and shielded it
from everything it didn't need shielding from, it spun away
bewildered, annoyed, maybe it was just a biological blip.

They will eat from your palm, but it's not like they want to,
pigeons on the other hand, gulls—
those lurchers are in it for the thrill.
Who do you think you are, leaving this place,
Vincent Gallo? Because this isn't Tucson and Toronto wasn't L.A.
and you're not a right-wing movie star yet.

And one day your heart will stop repeating itself
you'll be looking straight at it, whatever
is in that barn will have come for you, and then what?
I wondered. The cost of living, though, it's really good out here.

Keep Dying

In March there was a heatwave, not balmy
but a warm front moved in.
I wore a dress and my rubber boots to greet you.
Here, I said. *Here is a dying person.*

We watched the person dying, you smoked outside
and the person kept dying.
And you said *you should eat something*
I said *he can't eat anything, the dying person*

He can only keep dying.
You said *yeah* and I said *yeah.*
The dying person breathed and existed.
Soon it would be summer.

Liquidators

Some cleft-hoofed, hood-eyed calves
swine whose organs are just too malformed
you'd keep them but it's a waste
of feed.

The ashes of your youngest tied to your hip
a leather pouch, a skin sack carrying
flakes of bones, shards of breath
to the shops with you.

In Chernobyl, the liquidators went in.
One brought out a baby
that baby was okay, you'd call it
a keeper. Some became monsters, too many parts, too few, and so on.

Ours was okay, nice to look at
a horror of DNA
inside, they couldn't charge
his muscles, he was bright as can be though.

I breathed on his face
look, like this, I said
do it, I said. I carried him
in a box in my arms, covered in mossy lambskin, the skin of a mother
sheep's baby.

Prepping for the Apocalypse

In this test, forget everything you know
about survival
sew a razor in your pleats
for this occasion
run (there will be no way to get away unharmed,
this is a least-harm-possible kind of test)
if you see a gull you've gone too far
you'll be stuck
with something, we'll work that out
dress wounds
jab stuff into wounds
no blood-trail
go for a clot of mud
crouch, make
a bleating call
inhuman as you can
look back at
the glass ball of your youth
the sounds of your shepherd clipped by a sedan
before someone's father shot him, a polished
hunting rifle. Waxed? I swear I can smell it,
blat! Blat in that manner
if it's cold, breathe into the air
from the piss boggy earth
he will find us
and if he doesn't
we've failed.

Boundary

After Geoffrey Brock

The soft, snow-fattened hills passing
as a wraparound background, not so much simile
as another way to say
I've been here before.

Cows, field boundary fence, highway
gravemarkers. Netflix and Prime half emptied
the parishes. Shuttered arena snack bars—kids play
hockey in the towns now.

I get out of the car and lean at a fence to catch
my breath, it isn't to be caught. I look at the horse, white
in the white field. I look square at him.

We're both here, it's dusk, my heart beats too
fast. His eyes are big glass balls of dim
light and snow. He has nothing
for me. A brown horse trots away

from a barn, startles me, presses
a large calm face to the fence boards. They see I have nothing
for them and move along. Snow falls, the hoof-pocked snow,
snowed upon and snowed upon

again, silently. You wouldn't know it at all really
until the following day.

Ranch Style

Douglas fir, not a proper fir
(I read somewhere), lined the numbered streets,
once they were strewn with lights.
One stood in front of the church just over there.
The single mothers stacked
in two bedrooms near the stoplight, their trees
plastic and wire, their kids
tell them about the smell of the living rooms
in friends' suburban ranch-style homes
pine, sap, Christmas paper
Maybe the moms say, we'll get one next year
and a cat and a dog—
those houses have cats and dogs, the kids might say.
One year they get fish, one year
a used sedan, but mostly they buy oil
for the greedy tank to keep the red from the babies' noses,
the floors make them hop in the morning
but in no time they're warm enough.
There's milk and bread and fruit.
The fish swim in their bowl,
next year they'll get a real tree from the lot.

Straw Dog

There will be people
maybe they will be like people now
but better.

There will be fruit and death and Wi-Fi
so pretty much everything we have
now, but maybe better.

Most of us have seen one of us
dying, gasping, and so on
the same old ways, maybe death

will be more flamboyant
and we'll watch each other be killed
in a Peckinpah shootout.

Today we're an OHIP strain, tethered
husks of a person, IV'd for
the long haul. But who knows what will come.

Most have us have seen another one of us naked,
naked and weary
and eating a piece of fruit,

the trick is to do it while hooking up
a morphine line and counting breaths, expressing
breast milk, sending a text

<3 this only matters while we're alive.

The Dinner Guest

You are routed there but can't make it. A table
set like a bouquet of blood and earth,
a bouquet choked in the barrel
of a bayonet that only
the bloodied eye can see.
A house you haunted with youth, rooms schooled
by your hands (what did they see?)

You pull in, turn off your seat warmers.
The table is set—a boy
sits in your seat, tears into your meat
with his new incisors, wears
your buckskin pelt. A dog
barks, a mother scolds someone who spills
something. A man like your father stares like your father
into a glass. A girl asks for more.

You press your face to the window, an older boy
looks up, is he your brother? You can't make him out.
You call to him but your voice has no urgency.
Your eyes are useless here, you press harder
against the glass until it bursts against your pupil.
Bright light. Love. The clotted eye. Flash.

Breastfeeding Your Third-Born Through the Sixth Extinction While Your Boyfriend Attends Trial

Mothers looking each other up
and down, back up, blow
air fast out of nostrils.
Screw off, one says.

Sure, happy to.
One feeds her son from the breast,
draws ire. I do the same.
Dregs of my middle-class history

pursuing me even as I owe back rent.
In a courthouse built out of economic optimism
marble and pillars prop up
a roomful of Marys,

young girls who wait for their boyfriends
while sons of God
or other men rest in their arms. They search
for water, shake

powder formula into bottles
at the fountain, check their phones. Babies
eat chips in strollers. There is a week-old newspaper
says, apparently, this could all come to an end.

Cosmopolitan Distribution

You're making dinner, avoiding the sound
and staple-heavy since it'll be spring soon.
Months between you still but a sense of bloom
has its chokehold held, choked bore hounding your throat.

Step away it must be saying, *and make new,*
everyone suffers this sometime.
Spring, that gossamer tabloid of a season,
its miniature buds and immature loves.

Little deaths breaking free of soft blue eggshells,
little deaths forgotten and forgotten and the bare arms
of young girls (may they be remembered in winter's shrill drag),
their bare parts curious, catching at all and your man's eye,

a lake of open eyes, caught at last and all unravelling:
untold threads pulling free of the plucked birds squatting
at sprung drop-leaf tables.

Good

After Philip Larkin

How funny it is, tripping the curbs home,
stealing flowers from their soft, black beds.
Even the ruddy drunks falling
peacefully from doorways can see

that I know you love me and don't care. A pause
in decency, I'm a good girl but still too good
at making quick work of small talk
and fingering buttonholes to be very good.

It's hard to say: I'll never make love again, I'll never be lonesome
without sounding like a ready fool, but if I whisper it
to my husband while he sleeps at night
it sounds like all love, all beauty.

Handful

After Roddy Lumsden

I've handled myself on trains, been handled, roughhoused
by a housewife for being rough
and ready in the cabin of a ship and never thinking
Oh to love but hoping I'd finish,
finish before it stopped. And jerked

from our seats I'm sure I wasn't the first
to smell my hands, below, to taste what'd come
of three days or five days strange, country
unlike my own getting itself up and inside my T-shirt, linted
nipples and armpits, oh.

Spent my nights with a British boy (who hasn't?), who rolled
his shirtsleeves, buttoned down at night and read T.S. Eliot.
Who pawned a gun for a silverish ring, made me smell
like tobacco and, in the quiet, green-fingered morning
made me miss him like nobody's business.

And I've been called a handful, hard to live with, I'd make a shoddy
wife. Here in Canada graffiti rollers itself across pocked concrete
and a dozen *rock an' rolls* or *I loved Donnas.* There are local sayings
our foreign boys are still amusing themselves with, another wind-chill
    lark
and sometimes *life is great, isn't it darling?*

The Common Heart Attack

This heart stammers, its tick-tock's obsolete
as an alarm clock's second hand, on
and on (It must go) What happens, love? Something
pumps, explodes through something? A small elastic ball hammers
It isn't mine, which beats against the yoke-stir of joy
I might feel. The little heart thumps and the child
shifts, a duvet falls, creates a comic chaos
and like slapstick, this blasé-brute life quickens
and my fat heart is agile, slender limbs just handy
enough to make this alright. A big, uncouth moon
just is, not winking like his fleet of stars, not fleeting,
just is, its face sings I remember you little girl
the dark-eyed insomniac that kept a secret folded
beneath a pillow's cool underside,
a cigarette or love letter, a child's rotten tooth—I cannot recall.

Pastoral Tourism

Before the spring, summer, long-burrowed below,
swells. The sun's disciples team up
and storm the ugly roadsides
living only to bud and open and open,
to charm the bulge of tourists who might cut them down
and gild their wide brim hats. If you wait around forever
one of them will give you 20 dollars
to sit for a portrait and listen to long, dull tales
of what fun a girl can have if they'd only let loose
the ties from their ponytails.

St. Michael's

Last night you could walk into your neighbourhood
step over the flower tops and breathe
into the chests of the gone, poor souls,
bring life again, a pulse of blood and nerve
raging its joyful song like an ambulance—an abstract
bang of colour and light and music.
It's not true but you have a mile-wide dream streak
still waiting in your REM: the penknives and revolvers of your
boyhood,
racing horses and their cool, heavy purses.
Someone's watching the books of course,
someone's keeping the sheets tucked around your legs.

Homecoming

After Margaret Atwood

No one is weighing up a hook and an eye
(any hook, any eye) around here.
A ring finger and a babysitter,
at most. In these parts it's all the same:
a hole in the wall, in the ground, dug out
for what? In your table. You eat around it or
stick an umbrella through it, to keep
some character between you and the rest
of it. Lightness emptying into dark won't survive
the slow pitcher's pitch—thank god
you almost belonged here, once.
There is your basketball, your skis in the shed.
A canoe? Somewhere. The holes get deeper and big
as quarries and empty as some mines
until the next day and the next day
and so on. The tragedy lends itself to the modern machine:
a late car payment, a busted heart, a leaky condom
transforms into just something
that happened, like a key broken in a door
or a key that turned and did the job,
successfully. It's all the same.

Common Law

It takes some revolt to bring us together
now, a burglary, noise from without
we'll stay beside one another on fitted sheets
and wonder at the way we've domesticated
so that we excuse ourselves to turn
once again, reaching for a light switch in the dark
and even if we wanted to touch, it would be harder
than touching a stranger on a train
and who can blame us for reaching out here and there
across a desk or sofa to touch a hem or let a hem be touched?

Lorazepam Fact Sheet

You could be richer and thinner;
but you are not dead, girl.
Go get it, you deserve to feel seen.
Don't waste another diet cola day
being anything but a better you,
a calmer you, buffer
the sadness, forget to kill yourself.
Try on your swimsuit
and think, if it fits this snug
your ghost would be much too fat.
Be beautiful.
Remember when you gave up
smoking? Don't stress carcinogens right now
—get a pack. Don't text an ex.
But if you must, text an ex who choked you
like he meant it. Forget
about test results and take three pills,
or watch a song and dance picture about being in love.
Chill, baby girl. The side effects are all rare.
Self-care is everything.
You may find you are doing
much better now.

Shared Accommodations

I'd give my eye teeth for a moment
of quiet. But the eye roves—the eye,
wrist, thigh, whole heart.

The whole heart, blood-slick and heaving
as a cat, almost alive, packed
with buckshot: sodden and fat and horrifying.

The whole heart, thrashing
gracelessly, on. And just outside
of its understanding, the body—mindful

of nothing, slaughtering, fucking,
drinking, eating. My lonely selves, half-
brothers, sleeping in separate rooms.

Our Mothers

Once carried a dog-eared Tolstoy
in their bag. Hitchhiked out of little towns
to slightly bigger towns and worked
nights, studied and kept their hair neatly or not
neatly on top of their heads. Before they met our fathers.
And later sat passenger back to the smaller town,
got fatter and had babies and got '80s thin again.
Grimaced through half of their lives
so much so we thought
that was them smiling. So much so
you squint and hold the rectangular photograph closer
and ask your brother, is mom smiling here or crying?
Our mothers behind the cellophane, in wedding dresses, lighting
birthday candles, preferring one of us over another,
graduating, standing in pantsuits with their siblings at a family dinner
smiling or crying, we'll never know.

What Love

It takes its solace wherever it can:
a greeting card, corner store carnations.
But how will it survive the two of us?
Bludgeoned at our table, our headboard,

and where will it thrive
when we've muted its glory
with arrogance and lust, exploited, forsaken?
Asked, bloodied and pinned at last,

to pound and pulsate and march on
for two who cannot do for themselves.
I've had love like paper, folded and worn
and kept it safe like a bird, wing-bust,

in my pocket, and love that arrested
skepticism, begged for a God
and when it did not find God said,
Oh well, okay, who needs him anyway.

What love comes between us,
our forceful existence, and endures the skinned-raw heart,
beats on and when it cannot remember
our names, resumes and forgets to feel sore about it.

Life Choices

When you choose to die it is not respected like
being approved for a mortgage is respected.
When I got a car my neighbours were like,
hey, great car, I knew I had accomplished something, for them.

Dying is even greater, I told them,
my neighbours, one of them said, *do we know you from hockey?*
The others said things to the effect of, *it's defeat, it's as good as*
a broken fast. They buckle their L.L. Bean vests to the chin.

But I know better—I saw you draw in a whole galaxy of white
eyes and fingertips swirling 'round ever closer with each breath lost.

Plan Ahead

The space love cuts out
will need to be filled with loss.
Make room, pain is big.

Learning to Drive
(Notes from my driving instructor + my online yoga class)

A wet road mottled with leaves, the ratio
of red to yellow to orange uncanny. What's the probability
a deer will jump out and take to your hood
as a latchkey kid to television, but it happens.

Let go. Be present.

Don't slam on the brakes, it's bad for the brakes
and you will kill everyone, don't overreact, pull gently
to the shoulder, don't process the fear. A green new deal is no good
if the children of lawyers go out murdering all the animals.

Breathe, be a tree.

Take the light-dappled corners tight, hug them,
like a latchkey kid's kid to dairy allergies, like a Zennial
to a class-action glyphosate lawsuit. A wide corner endangers
cyclists, other vehicles, your insurance premiums

could go up. Be light. Neglect gravity. The future
is whatever we can afford for it to be.

For Moses or Almost Anyone

The longest con is
Earth looping the sun again
never to be home.

Rationing Fruit

Press against what's rotted
beneath the peel, soft, sweeter and no one
wants it.

The skin glows under the fluorescent light as though it's not hiding
death. A stem sits loose in the cloven part,
muted brown, resting really.

Like a mother on a drip in
chemo—her wig and potions (plucked
from a satiny makeup bag) hustling some beauty back from death.

Single Mothers in Mid-Late 2000s Parkette

We sat on one of those park benches,
a flock of gulls intruded
on our silence.

I was two pregnancies deep.
You weren't leaving
or joining anyone (you said).

That wasn't what I meant
whether it was or wasn't
I can't remember now.

We drank coffee from Rabba.
The winter was hard. You wrote from Montreal,
nothing from Berlin, sent a pic from Montauk.

The next time I see you it's winter again.
You put the baby in the stroller while I dress. We walk
along St. Mary and stand under some stone

arch or another. University girls laugh. The baby sleeps.
You get a text from your girlfriend. Neither of us has heard
from our fathers in some time.

This is an approximation. I don't remember details,
only that the city has changed, the baby is bigger.
The winters are still hard on everyone.

High and Low

When you first stopped breathing I ran
yelling something blue
and calling for help in a language I didn't know. Your brain
wasn't damaged in the commotion—was I relieved?
Sure I was. Next time you stopped they were close by, they had
everything someone so breath-broke could want,
even a vaccum for your throat, then after that I had it,
the vacuum, a machine and a mask I could lay
against your skin and pretend I was saving you and imagine
it gave you life. We pretended for the better part of two months,
you doing the thing where you could not get oxygen, me
holding a paper mask, light as a Japanese fan
breathing air through its ridiculous tubes at us, your face
pale as a painted geisha accepting the mask, for my
sake. When you stopped finally it was because I let you,
at last. There was a movie on, Kurosawa, that's why
I make the fan comparison, the one where the boy is taken,
the wrong boy. We watched it together, you dying, me
with the mask. Tall grass, the black and white mountains.

Women Sleeping with Men

My girlfriends lie across the used IKEA couches all over the city
while men return messages on a balcony. They lean into
each other for months, stand like two bottles of milk on a stoop,
slouched on benches, text from Russian bathhouses.
Maybe he's done too much Iranian blow.
Maybe she emails from a bedroom where a child has a fever.

Nevermind, it was fine, you were fine. They were fine.
They would not disrupt each other's lives. Someone
would leave the city forever and the other would
text on someone else's balcony.

The Late 2000s

It is what it is, right? My neighbour
asked me. *Yeah, yeah, totally.*
I waited until the blackest pitch of night
to walk. The lake cracked, a racoon
looked over a shoulder at me.
Snow sat on ice and ice on water,
my soles somewhere above. If it was a new year
no one told me, nothing changed.
Prehistoric air, frozen and thoughtless,
without thought, entered my parted lips.
The trees stood as they did, the hunters tucked
in, their rifles asleep in cabinets. Tomorrow I will work.
My kids will ask for things,
my hands will hurt, the lake cracks,
the snow falls on ice. Water rushes somewhere deeper.
My neighbour will have something to say
to me about the new New Year.

Advice from Homesteaders Online: Prepping for the Event

It's not going to happen like you think, a jar of apples
bathed in water, sealed with wax will get you through
many days, I can't say how many but we'll make enough. Costco
has mac and cheese, like a barrel,
lasts 18 years give or take, imagine
being with someone that long? Anyway I don't eat dairy.
I'm learning how to build fires
and strip things, de-feather, de-bone,
un-life things, de-breathe them.
When the event occurs, they say
it'll be people like me
who know these things, who have apples
who may or may not know you anymore
who will really be living their best life.

Mere Extinction

After the world is burned up and all of the poor
countries are wiped out and the animals scarce
you'll kill to hear these sounds.
A fetid paw: food. The screech and wing patter:
protein. In the end it will be better
to be here.

The possibility of compost scraps, a whole
cantaloupe sways a racoon from the trusses, a rat
but it wasn't a rat, an opossum rather—playing
dead or dead, mostly trying not to die.
The mice, reckoning with faulty
DNA—heart attacks in live traps
(you may as well take them out
with a shovel and be done with it).

All life, your life, all of it was
muted here. When the burn ban's up though maybe a spell
cast out of drywall dust and broken
Tinder dates, thyme
and essential oil (improvise if you must),
a bundle of twigs and a lighter will do the trick.

This place won't get any easier
is what the guy at the municipal office keeps telling you,
the animals will dig that garden up if you won't trap them. And
there is
no magic to be had in the here and now.

But when it rains here, old glass pill bottles
wash clear beneath the spouts and when the sun strikes,
none of that—the Bornean orangutan,
the burning people, your old self, mere
extinction—will have anything
on their light.

Meat Eaters

The first time I ate meat I was done having babies
but you wanted to give me a part of the life cycle
somehow. You carved the deer's flesh from the deer's bones and
    promised
if I ate it I would survive the year. I would come
to terms with eating the deer, it was the fawn
we swallowed, our knees drenched in blood, the rudderless eye
of this deer's child, blindsided by your expression
of love—emptied of anything
lifelike—if I didn't say this already, this was a dream.
It didn't matter how much I thanked the milk-eyed carcass
it would taste how it tasted and it would be dead from now on.
Blood filled my mouth and I saw I was wrong about it mattering
or not and the deer life flooded me and I was made for this world
at last and for the first time, in the dream, I breathed
and was at home with it all.

Shechita

After Irving Layton

Poets, other poets
I read know about hunger,
its quiet violence. The poem

starves as you do.
Its mouth a metaphor
for work.

Its sin: vanity, skipping
form and telling
too much.

Repent like today
is the Sabbath of Sabbaths, cut
its throat, bleed it out.

Let it be born again, a slick
new thing into the world. Its breath
fresher, its mouth open

in hunger, in brutality,
its everyday tongue. It doesn't
need to rhyme.

Pilgrimage

We took what we could carry.
Flee, flee, said everyone.
We did. My fingernails were bloody.
We carried our babies, dead, living, womb-ridden.

We learned to grow food here.
I never touched a man again.
The air was clean, the poison wasn't evident.
The air was good.

If we stopped moving, stopped pulling weeds, let our hands
heal, you could hear them at the door, hear them coming for us.
If you slept a wink, the blood would swell from your nail beds
and our milk would go sour in our babies' mouths.

Losing Avraham

When I lost him
he wasn't lost, a goner,
it is a misleading title.

It took years, losing him.
Our buffer was bad connections,
children's recitals,
a red letter year at work.

I sometimes wished we'd never met.
It became clear a knife
resting agreeably in a drawer
was crueller than one in the sunlight.

In time photographs disappeared
from the fridge freezer door.
We forgot to celebrate, things
moved to any day you can make it.

We stopped making it.
And it was okay, good
even, I drove by the cave of the patriarchs.
I didn't recognize the way

he had the garden laid out. Maybe it wasn't his garden,
and it hadn't gone like this. Maybe this too is a literary construct.

Shroud

Long days passed me, I slept
through a year of winter days. Someone
fed the hens, though I hear they don't need it, someone
fed the babies, they're alive.

I'd spent a good season canning so it wouldn't be trouble
when I decided to sleep. Spring was a small ache
in my ribcage, leftover from girlhood almost loud enough
to wake anything.

A few dark-eyed juncoes pushed
their beaks at the melted snow
looking for more of what they needed, a barn
cat trotted habitually, forward.

A child tugged at my nightgown or pillowcase
crawled against me and held my wrist for a pulse.

Nightingale Song

A mouthful of teeth and tongue,
bloodful lung, pocket steep
with Ativan.
Overdrawn throatful of desire
for oxygen, time, mother's milk.

A snide nurse's flirty nails sing:
tap tap tap tap tap tap tap tap tap tap tap.
A trust-fund doctor
(red-shirted, silverspooning
fraternity vibes) splits a smoke with me behind an ambulance,
tells okay jokes, kills the time.

Oh, all these ones in this room are dying,
the child in the third bed has so many balloons
you'd think it was having a birthday ever again.
The humour gets dryer than a first wife in menopause
(the doctor's jokes rub off on you).

Your child knows you and you know him and neither of you knows
death. *Rat a tat tat tap tap tap*, earfuls of blood, a palm
pushing back at a syringe,
being alone, buried alive, dreaming, together
checking your pocket for pills.

Begging the bitter nurse for a cot,
duck the doctor tap tap tap.
Rat a tat tat, hospital flowers, the baby's breath, kiss the mouth, breathe
into him. Look up because
you've looked everywhere else.

Where the Otonabee Meets Rice Lake

The children in the villages were told to go out.
Some trudged too close to the calves and were sought,
they ran in plastic bagged boots, jumped
over barbed wire, snagged by the cold, metallic thump of the
    electric fence
and the poplars. Others slipped through the lake ice
where we tossed buttered bread at ducks in summer.
It was their mothers who found them looking good enough
for open caskets. Some kept running, branches struck
wide open eyes, they kept on
through the brush, grazed
by nettles, they would release
some kinds of poisons, if they could, but
they hadn't time, the balsam
poplars snapping back at them, the pale birch, their cool
trunks like so many bodies I've never seen
like cool silent bodies, a forest thick with them
a burst of geese above form a V, a bold new Luftwaffe in the sky.

New Zealand Doomsday Bunker

Be prepared.
Prepare your skin with sunlight,
increase this over weeks.

By the time we get to New Zealand
the people back home will be taking KI pills
gathered around a crank radio.

The cell towers will be down,
the rain barrels empty.
They'll have eaten through their food supply.

I feel sad to think of it
but we cannot all achieve the same glory
as the elite minded.

I skinned and gutted my animals on day one.
I packed the canned goods, water tablets
while you were still waiting for an emergency broadcast.

It's not as though you don't deserve to live,
you just weren't made to, we're told.
When he comes he will lead us all

to New Zealand, we'll eat fruit
like gods, and the taste of blood
will be washed away.

And the water will be pure
and we'll make babies and teach them
concealed carry and sun protection.

Becoming Mike Tyson

To begin I should ask him how he became himself.
How did he get a new face, when did he decide
Mao was the light, to stop eating meat, start speaking to me?

When I overheard the neurologist cracking jokes
and asking, is it policy to wait for the test results to tell me you
were going to die,
I blinked and your dead body was resting on my arms, and my arms,
my face, my heart, my chest holding my heart, my face—my face

wanted to be a new face. And the words, the beeping
beeps and the flowers that filled my flat were shrill
and burned me alive—I wished. I was still there.

And I had to find a way to tattoo
a new face over this face I had
when I pretended I didn't know you were dying.
(I knew it from the second you were born!)

I found several articles, quizzes re: creating a new and better me.
I lay in bed with magazines, the abyss and me in a staring contest,
I thought about how I could hear words and see things and suffer
through not being burned alive.

How did you decide on the Che one, Mao Zedong, Arthur Ashe,
Monica
Turner (was it love)? Why the '90s tribal one, are you
better now, what is a fair punishment
for the things I have done (and is this place prison enough)?

I DM'd the hell out of every Mike Tyson account hoping
you would tell me what to do. But you wouldn't say.
Eventually I got word from Mike Tyson Fans of North America:
    "Evie, a revolution is not a dinner party" and I took that as a sign
I was doing everything right and everything would be okay.

Acknowledgements

Thank you to my dear family and friends.

Thank you ECW Press, my editors Michael Holmes and Emily Schultz, and thank you to Alex Porco.